The Best Book of Sharks

Claire Llewellyn

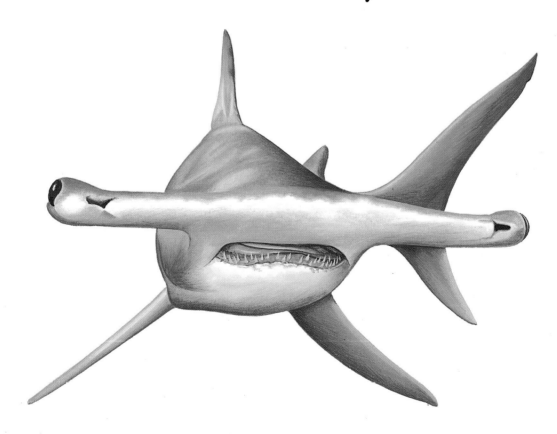

KINGFISHER

NEW YORK

Contents

Author: Claire Llewellyn
Consultant: Brian Harris, London
  Zoo Aquarium
Senior editor: Sarah Milan
Editor: Sue Nicholson
Designer: Malcolm Parchment
Production controller: Caroline
  Jackson
Illustrators: Ray Grinaway,
  Roger Stewart

KINGFISHER
Larousse Kingfisher Chambers Inc.
80 Maiden Lane
New York, New York 10038
www.kingfisherpub.com

First published in 1999
10 9 8 7 6 5 4

1SC/0601/WKT/(MA)/128KMA

LIBRARY OF CONGRESS CATALOGING-IN-PUBLICATION DATA
Llewellyn, Claire.
  The best book of sharks / by Claire Llewellyn.—1st ed.
    p. cm.
  Published simultaneously under the title: My best
book of sharks.
  Includes index.
  Summary: Introduces the world of sharks, examing
their characteristics, breeding, life cycle, and behavior
and describing various species.
  1. Sharks Juvenile literature. [1. Sharks.] I. Title.
QL638.9.L57 1999
597.3—dc21 99-12760 CIP

ISBN 0-7534-5173-5 (hb)
ISBN 0-7534-5429-7 (pb)
Printed in Hong Kong/China

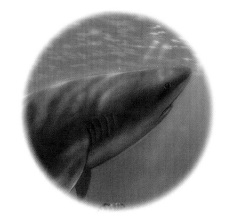

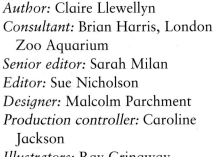

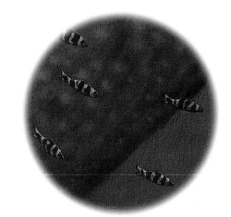

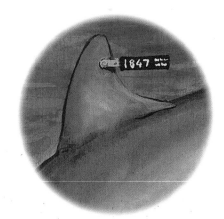

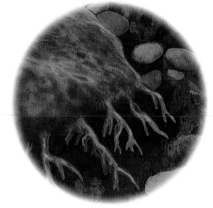

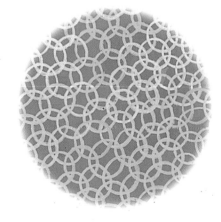

Meet the shark

The shark is one of the fastest fish in the sea. Every part of its body is perfect for the water—its light, flexible skeleton, its smooth, sleek shape, and its powerful fins and tail. These features mean some sharks are deadly hunters. Not all sharks are fast and fierce, though. Some, such as the whale shark, are gentle giants that feed only on the tiniest creatures in the sea.

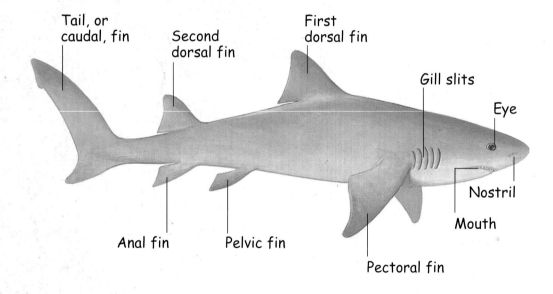

Tail, or caudal, fin

Second dorsal fin

First dorsal fin

Gill slits

Eye

Nostril

Mouth

Pectoral fin

Pelvic fin

Anal fin

A shark's body

Most fish have skeletons made of hard bone, but a shark's skeleton is made of light, flexible cartilage. This allows the shark to twist and turn very quickly. Like all fish, sharks use their gills to take in oxygen from the water.

Gray reef shark hunting for prey over a coral reef

A world of sharks

There are about 375 kinds of sharks, and they are many different colors, shapes, and sizes. Many sharks are sleek and slim. Others are flabby and flat. Some are silver-gray. Others are brown, blue, spotted, or striped. Many sharks are darker on top and paler underneath. This is called countershading. It makes a shark much harder to spot—both from below, when it is seen against the light, and from above, against the murky sea.

Pygmy shark
(8 in. long)

Cookiecutter shark
(20 in. long)

Dogfish
(16-24 in. long)

Wobbegong shark
(4 ft. long)

Sawshark
(4.5 ft. long)

Port Jackson shark
(5 ft. long)

Frilled shark
(6.5 ft. long)

Leopard shark
(6 ft. long)

Angelshark
(4 ft. long)

Blue shark
(10.5 ft. long)

Lemon shark
(11.5 ft. long)

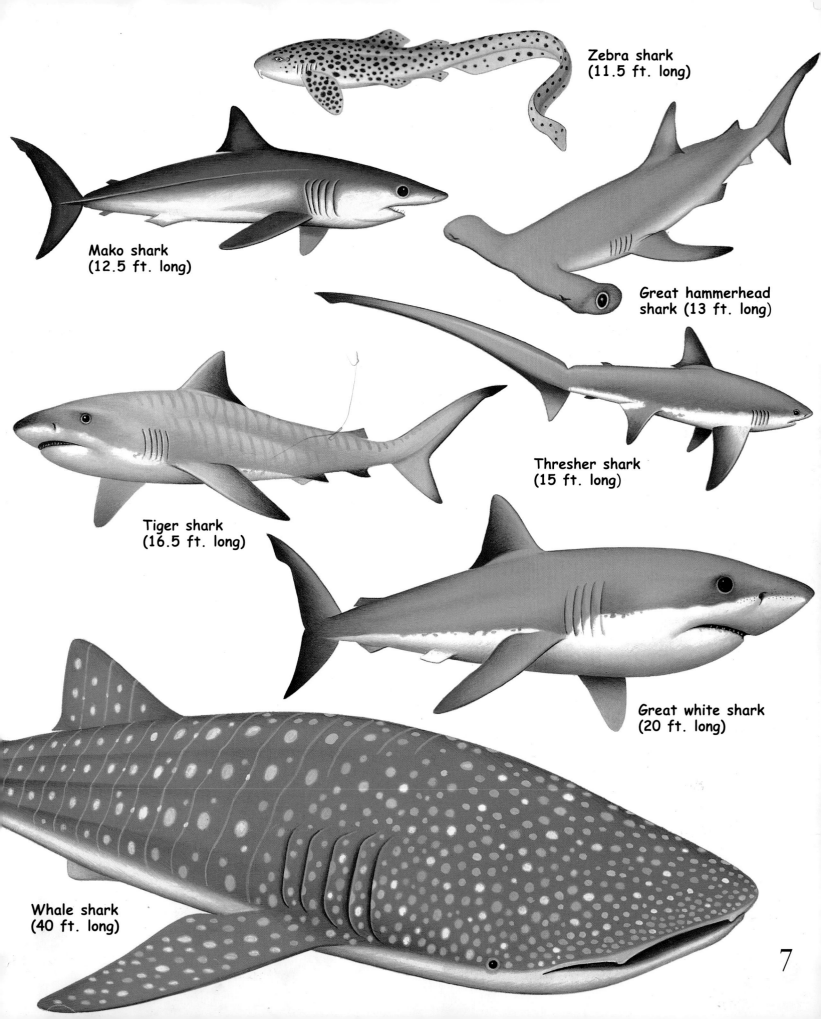

Zebra shark
(11.5 ft. long)

Mako shark
(12.5 ft. long)

Great hammerhead
shark (13 ft. long)

Thresher shark
(15 ft. long)

Tiger shark
(16.5 ft. long)

Great white shark
(20 ft. long)

Whale shark
(40 ft. long)

7

Swimming champions

A shark hardly seems to move as it swims along. It simply flicks its tail from side to side to push its body through the water. It uses its fins to turn, stop, rise, or dive. Most fish have soft, bendable fins that can be stretched out or tucked back. A shark's fins are stiff and stick out like paddles, and cannot be folded away.

Gray smooth hound sharks swimming along the seabed

Shark skin

Most sharks' skin is covered with tiny, thorny teeth called denticles. If you stroked the skin from back to front, it could cut your hand.

Shark tails

Shark tails have different shapes. Bull and thresher sharks have long, streamlined tails that slice through the water so that the sharks can twist and turn quickly. The swell shark's broader tail gently wafts the water so that the fish can cruise along the seabed. The balanced shape of the great white's tail allows it—and others like it—to swim the fastest of all.

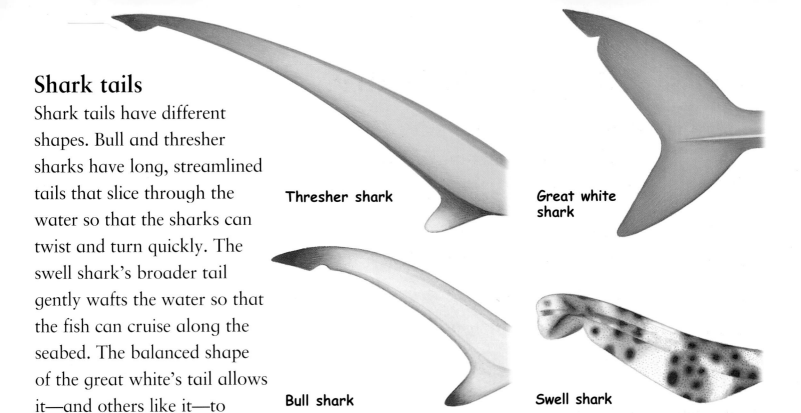

Thresher shark

Great white shark

Bull shark

Swell shark

Baby sharks

Baby sharks are known as pups, and they grow in different ways. Most grow from eggs in their mother's body, and are born into the sea. Others grow from eggs that are laid in the water. Each egg sits in a case, which hardens to protect the growing pup. The shark hatches out when it is almost fully grown, and swims off to hide somewhere safe. It must then take care of itself—the mother leaves it on its own.

Hammerhead shark pups

Born into the sea

Shark pups slip out through an opening in their mother's body. They are joined to their mother by tiny cords, which break as the pups swim away.

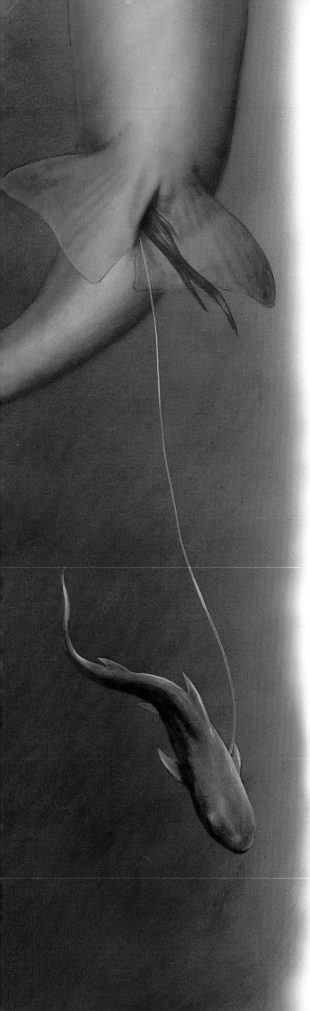

Lemon shark pups

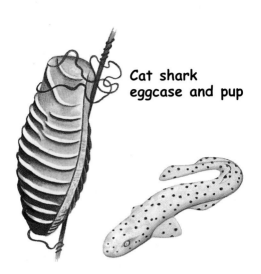

Cat shark eggcase and pup

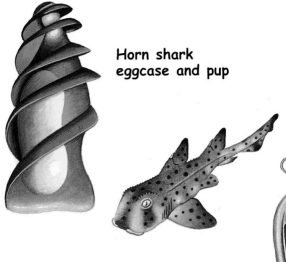

Horn shark eggcase and pup

Dogfish eggcases (also called mermaid's purses)

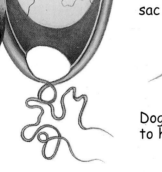

Shark eggcases

Eggcases are tough and built to last. A cat shark's eggcase has tiny tendrils that cling tightly to plants.

A horn shark's eggcase survives in cracks in the rocks. Other eggcases settle on the seabed. Many are eaten before the pups hatch.

Tendrils of cat shark's eggcase wraps around plant

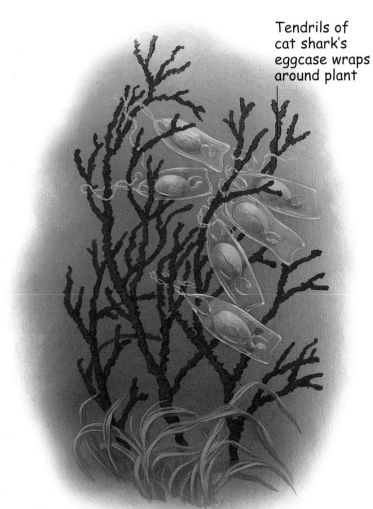

Dogfish pup (4 in. long)

Yolk sac

Dogfish ready to hatch

Dogfish eggs

Dogfish lay about 20 eggs, often in a clump of seaweed. Each egg contains a yolk sac for the pup to feed on as it grows. The eggs take nine months to hatch. The pups look just like their parents, but smaller.

11

Homing in

Sharks are very good at finding their prey in the vast, dark world of the ocean. They can feel movement in the water from far away. They can smell the faintest whiff of blood. They can even pick up the electrical signals from an animal's beating heart. Most sharks prefer to hunt alone, but sometimes a group will attack the same prey. The sharks snap wildly and even bite one another in a savage feeding frenzy.

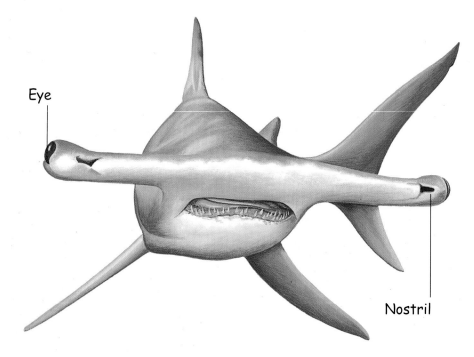

Eye

Nostril

Hammerhead hunter

A hammerhead shark has an eye and a nostril on each end of its hammer-shaped head. As it swims, it swings its head from side to side to pick up signals from the water.

Gray reef sharks attack a tuna in a feeding frenzy

The deadly jaws

Sharks feed on nearly every creature in the sea. They catch penguins, seals, turtles, fish, and crabs. Because different kinds of sharks feed on different kinds of food, they have different-shaped jaws and teeth. A few teeth drop out during every meal, but new ones move up to take their place. A shark goes through hundreds of teeth during its lifetime.

Shaken to pieces

Sharks cannot chew. If a meal is too large to swallow whole, they shake it from side to side to tear it into chunks.

Ragged teeth

The sandtiger shark (also known as the ragged tooth or gray nurse shark) has several rows of sharp, spiky teeth. Each tooth is about 1.5 inches long.

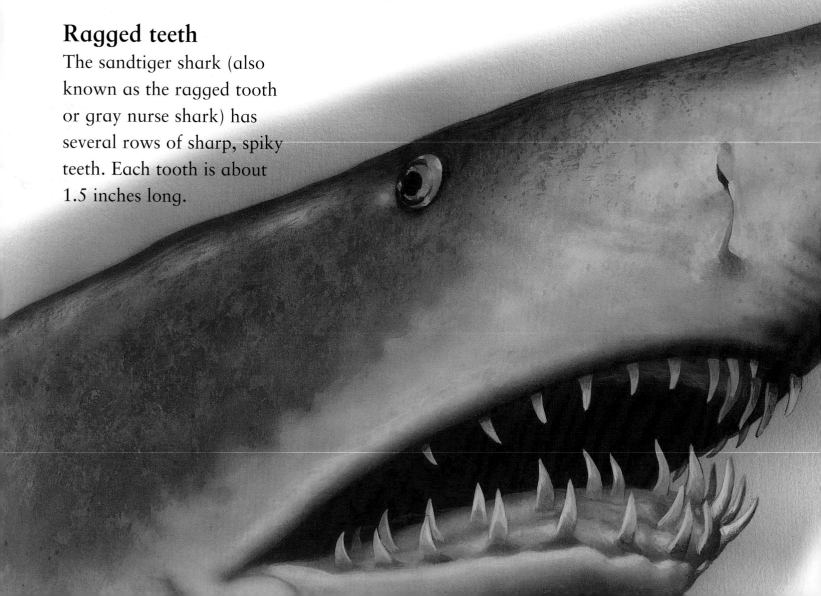

Types of teeth

A shark's teeth are a toolkit for catching and cutting up food. Long, spiky teeth can skewer a slithery octopus or squid. Serrated teeth can saw through bony fish. Hard, flat teeth can grind up shellfish, such as lobsters and crabs, and even crunch through a tough turtle shell.

Seal

Octopus

Squid

Spiked tooth—
mako shark, lemon shark

Pointed tip

Bony fish

Serrated and pointed tooth—
tiger shark, great white shark,
swell shark, bull shark

Crab

Lobster

Grinding teeth—
Port Jackson shark,
nurse shark

Turtle

Sea
urchin

Sandtiger shark
(10 ft. long)

Cookiecutter
shark

Lips form a round
sucker that grabs
hold of prey

A cookiecutter bite

A cookiecutter shark's jaws are perfectly round, like a cookie cutter. When it sinks its teeth into a seal or whale, it tears out a cookie-shaped mouthful.

15

Gentle giants

The whale shark is the world's biggest fish, yet it feeds on minuscule creatures. As the shark cruises along near the surface of the ocean, it sucks in great mouthfuls of water. This pours through curtains of long, fine bristles that hang inside the shark's mouth. The bristles work like a filter or sieve, trapping schools of plankton and tiny fish, which the shark then swallows.

Whale shark teeth

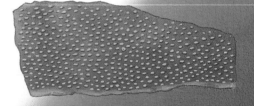

Tiny teeth

Whale and basking sharks have tiny teeth, about half the size of your little fingernail. They do not use them to bite or crush their food, but to help them spit it out from time to time.

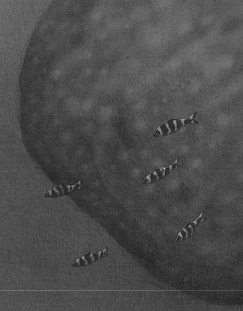

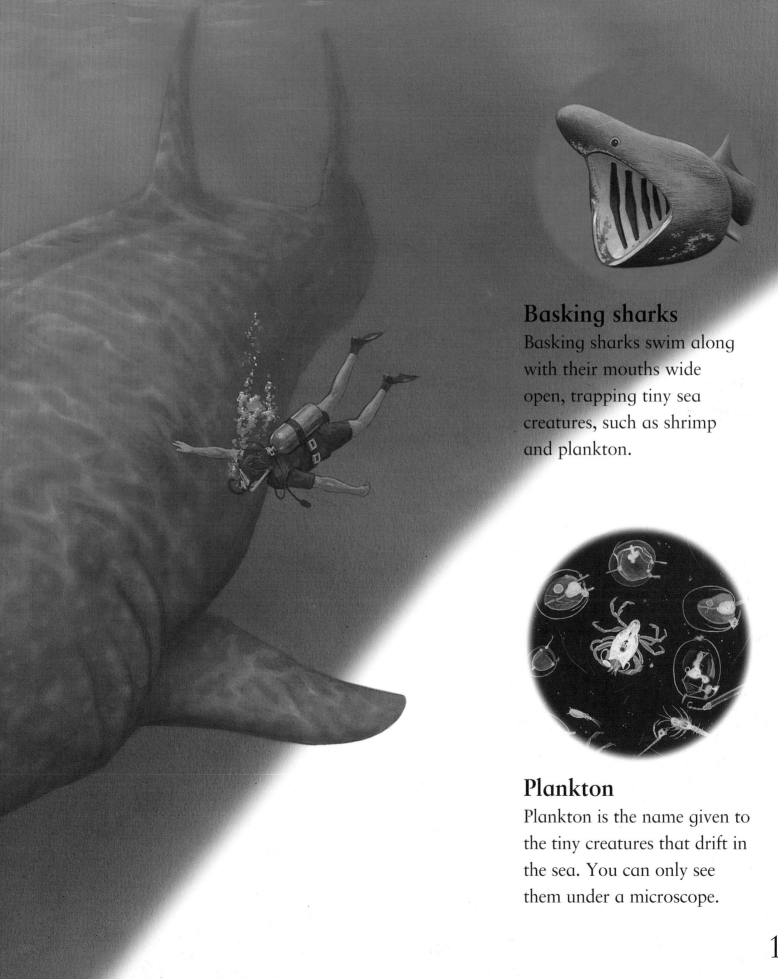

Basking sharks

Basking sharks swim along with their mouths wide open, trapping tiny sea creatures, such as shrimp and plankton.

Plankton

Plankton is the name given to the tiny creatures that drift in the sea. You can only see them under a microscope.

Sharks on the seabed

Some sharks hide at the bottom of the sea to rest or pounce on their prey. Their flat bodies, brown skin, and blotchy markings help them blend in with the stones and sand. One shark, the wobbegong, has frills of skin around its mouth. These look so much like pieces of seaweed that small fish swim up to nibble them and end up being eaten themselves.

Taking a break

Port Jackson sharks like to feed at night. They spend the day resting in sandy caves or in gaps between the rocks.

The wobbegong
shark waiting for
its next meal

Angel in the sand

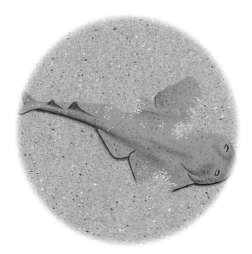

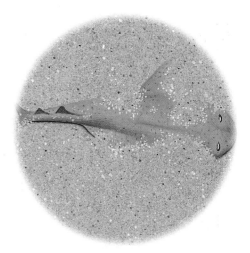

1 The angelshark spends much of its life resting and feeding on the seabed.

2 It flaps its fins to cover itself with sand. It is now almost invisible.

3 Its eyes are on the top of its head so that it can stay on the lookout for food.

Luminous sharks

Some sharks that live in deep, dark water have special ways of using light. The massive mouth of a megamouth shark shines with a silvery glow. This may attract the tasty schools of plankton that megamouths like to eat. The cookiecutter shark also uses light. Its belly glows a luminous green. This may attract a nearby animal, such as a whale, that is large enough to bite.

Bright lanterns

Lantern sharks swim in large schools. Each fish is covered with a luminous slime that glows in the dark. Scientists believe that this glowing slime may help the fish keep their place in the school.

Megamouth sharks live in such deep water that only six or so have ever been found

20

Shark attack!

Some sharks can be dangerous to humans. About 30 kinds of sharks, including the bull shark, tiger shark, and great white shark, have attacked people in the water. Some have even overturned sailboats. Large, meat-eating sharks have powerful jaws, and when they attack they often kill. However, shark attacks are very rare. There are only about 100 every year. You are much more likely to be struck by lightning than to be attacked by a shark.

DO: Tuck legs up and keep as still and quiet as possible

DON'T: Shout, splash, or kick legs in the water

Safety at sea

If someone falls overboard into the sea, they should not shout, splash, or kick their legs in the water. Sharks are attracted to noise and movement, and may mistake a splashing person for a school of fish.

Seal or surfer?

Sharks don't seem to like the taste of people. They do not usually eat people they attack.

Perhaps they bite swimmers by mistake—after all, from under the water, a surfer looks a lot like a seal.

Sea drama

Sound travels a long way under water. The noise of people splashing in the sea and the whirr of a rescue helicopter's rotor blades may attract sharks from several miles away.

Sharks in danger

Every year, about 100 million sharks are killed. Most of them are killed for their skin, meat, and fins. Some are killed for sport. Others are killed by accident when they swim into fishing nets or shark nets. Some kinds of sharks take years to have young, or may have only one pup a year. If more sharks die than are born each year, they will become extinct.

Made from sharks

Sharks are killed to make creams, medicines, and shark fin soup. Most of these goods can be made using other products.

Death trap

Harmless sharks are sometimes killed in nets put up to protect swimmers from more dangerous sharks.

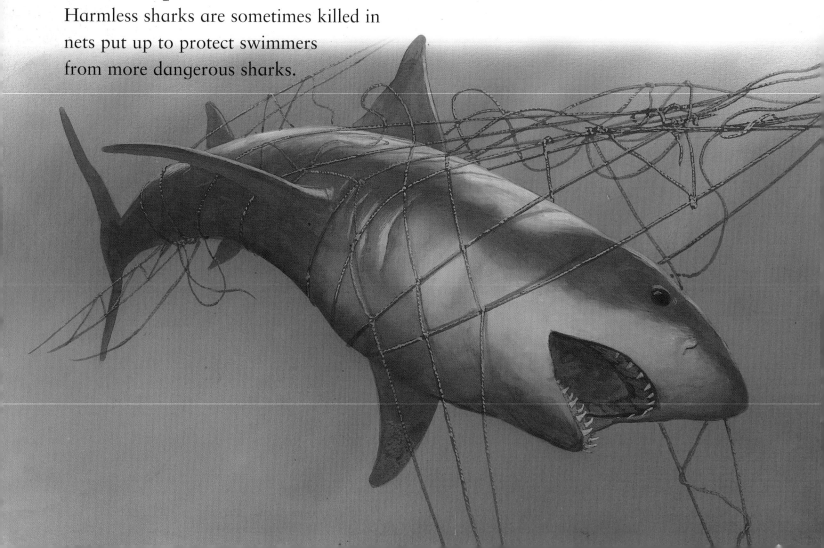

Shark fin soup is popular in many Asian countries.

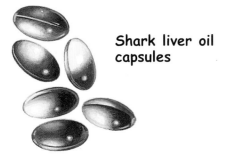

Shark liver oil capsules

Skin cream

Lipstick

A shark-tooth necklace is believed to give the wearer strength.

A sporting chance?

Some fast-swimming sharks, such as the mako shark, are the "big game" of the sea.

In the past, many sharks were killed for sport. Nowadays, anglers are encouraged to release them instead.

Studying sharks

Scientists still have many questions about sharks. How long do they live? How fast do they grow? How far do they swim? To help find the answers, scientists clip sonic tags to sharks' fins. The tags give out signals that the scientists can follow. Over the years, scientists have studied thousands of sharks, and are learning more about them. And the more they know, the better chance they have of saving them from extinction.

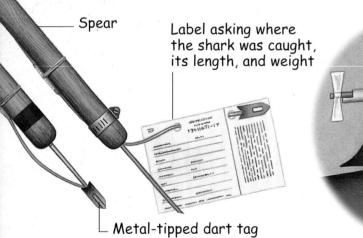

Spear

Label asking where the shark was caught, its length, and weight

Metal-tipped dart tag

Shark tags

Scientists use long spears to tag sharks in the water. A tag's label asks any angler who catches the shark to send in information about it.

Shark speedometer

Sometimes a tiny propeller is tied to a shark's dorsal fin. The propeller measures how fast the shark moves as it cruises through the sea.

Tagging a shark

Tagging is harmless to sharks as long as it is done quickly. In the long run, it may help protect them from extinction.

Shark gear

Many divers like to swim with sharks. They have to protect themselves in case they are attacked. Most divers wear special suits made of metal mesh. Some swim inside plastic scooters. To watch or photograph more dangerous sharks, divers stay inside a metal cage. They tie a bag of bait to the bars of the cage— then all they have to do is wait!

Bag of fish for bait

Steel cage

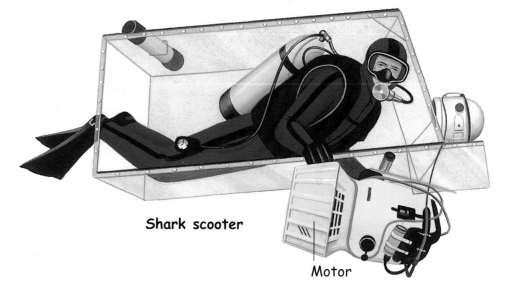

Shark scooter

Motor

Scary but safe

Sharks are attracted by metal, but a steel cage won't break even if it is rammed by a great white shark.

Plastic scooter

This shark scooter is made of strong, clear plastic. The diver can see well and move around freely.

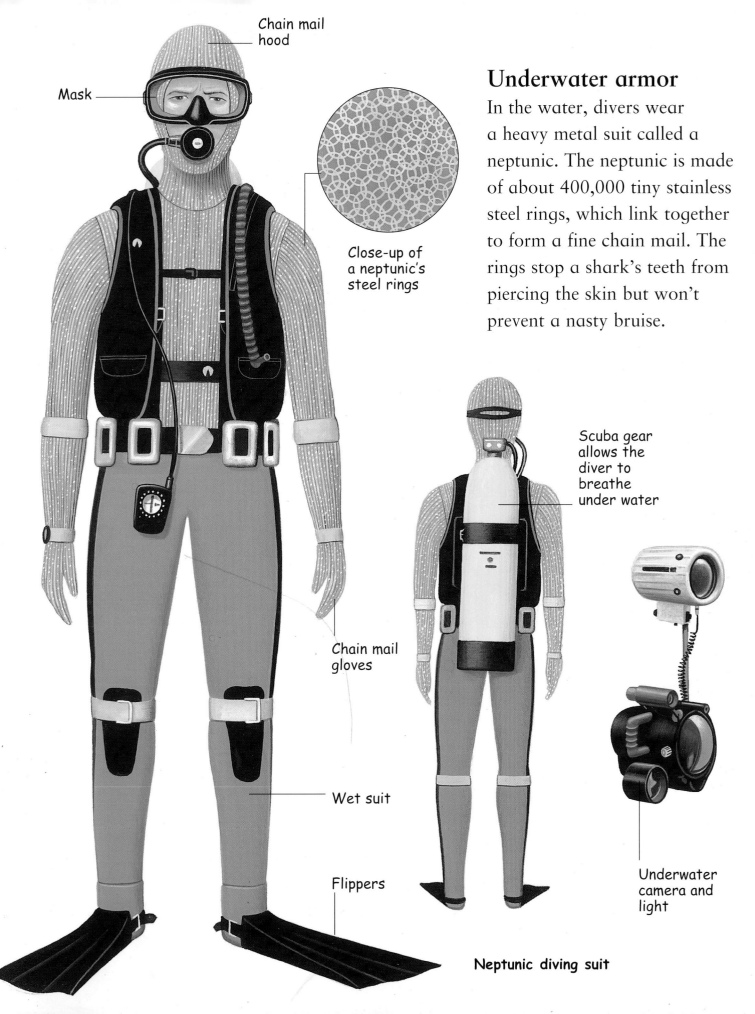

Chain mail hood

Mask

Underwater armor

In the water, divers wear a heavy metal suit called a neptunic. The neptunic is made of about 400,000 tiny stainless steel rings, which link together to form a fine chain mail. The rings stop a shark's teeth from piercing the skin but won't prevent a nasty bruise.

Close-up of a neptunic's steel rings

Scuba gear allows the diver to breathe under water

Chain mail gloves

Wet suit

Flippers

Underwater camera and light

Neptunic diving suit

29

Seeing sharks

You don't have to get wet to see a shark! You can watch one at an aquarium through a wall of glass. Why not sketch, make notes about, or photograph the different kinds of sharks you see? Of course, an aquarium is too small for large, fast sharks. These fish need a lot of space and are much better off in the open sea.

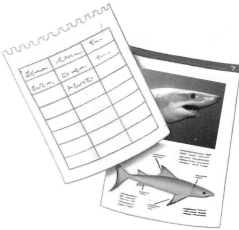

Making a shark factfile, with notes, photographs, and sketches

An all-around view

Some aquariums have ocean tanks big enough to house a whole coral reef. As visitors walk through glass tunnels, they enjoy an amazing view of different kinds of sharks, such as smooth hounds, sandtigers, or whitetip reef sharks.

Glossary

cartilage The rubbery or gristly material that forms a shark's skeleton.

coral reef A long line of coral that lies below the water in warm, shallow parts of the sea. Coral is built by tiny animals.

countershading The name given to the shading on sharks and many other fish. The darker back and paler belly make them harder to see, either from above looking down into deep, dark water, or from below, looking up toward bright sunlight.

denticles The small, stiff, thorny scales that make up a shark's rough skin.

extinct No longer living on Earth. An animal becomes extinct when none of its kind is alive.

feeding frenzy The activity that takes place among feeding sharks. They become excited, biting at anything.

fish An animal with a backbone that lives in water and breathes through gills. There are about 24,620 known kinds of fish. Some live in freshwater; some in saltwater. Some, such as the bull shark, can live in both.

gill The part of a fish's body that allows it to breathe under water. Gills take in oxygen from the water. Most fish have gills that are covered with flaps of skin, but sharks just have slits.

luminous Giving out a bright light.

neptunic A diving suit made of thousands of small steel rings. Divers wear a neptunic to protect themselves from sharks.

oxygen A gas that all living things need in order to survive. Oxygen is found in both air and water.

plankton Microscopic plants and animals that live in the sea.

predator A hunter.

prey An animal hunted by another for food.

pup A baby shark.

school a large group of one kind of fish.

scuba gear Equipment that includes an air tank and a breathing mask that lets divers breathe under water.

serrated Having a sharp, zigzag edge like a saw or steak knife.

skeleton The frame inside an animal's body that holds it up. Most fish have a bony skeleton, but a shark's skeleton is made of flexible cartilage.

streamlined Having a smooth body shape that moves easily through the water.

31

Index

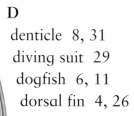